For my favorite cousins,
Ian and Ruth Fingerman—*F.S.*

For the adorable Christopher Fenton—*S.W.*

TODDLER TIME

by Francesca Simon
illustrated by Susan Winter

Orchard Books
New York

Orchard Books, A Grolier Company, 95 Madison Avenue, New York, NY 10016

Manufactured in Italy Book design by Tracey Cunnell
The text of this book is set in 20/28 Baskerville Schoolbook.
The illustrations are watercolor.

1 3 5 7 9 10 8 6 4 2

Library of Congress Cataloging-in-Publication Data
Simon, Francesca.
Toddler time / written by Francesca Simon ; illustrated by Susan Winter.
p.   cm.
Summary: A collection of illustrated poems that capture the many facets of a toddler's life.
ISBN 0-531-30251-2 (alk. paper)
1. Toddlers Juvenile poetry. 2. Children's poetry, English.
[1. Toddlers Juvenile poetry. 2. Toddlers Poetry. 3. English Poetry.] I. Winter, Susan, ill. II. Title.
PR6069.I4146T64   2000   821′.914—dc21   99-32942

Contents

WHEN I WAS ONE

When I was 1, I never cried.

When I was 2, I never lied.

When I was 3, I was never scared.

When I was 4, I always shared.

Well, almost always.

CHOOSING MY OWN CLOTHES

Today is the day!
Mom says I can choose—
I can decide what to wear.
Shall I dress as a fairy,
all white and airy?
Or shall I be brown as a bear?

Purple pirates are fun,
though it's hard to run
with a clanking sword by your side.
I could be a queen
with my cloak of green,
but I might get it stuck on the slide.

I love everything blue
from my hat to my shoe,
but now I'm not sure what to wear.
A frilly peach skirt?
A striped red shirt?
A yellow bow in my hair?

I know! Black boots are best—
I'll rush to get dressed
in my gold socks all shiny and new.
I'll grab a red ribbon,
a pink, and a blue.
Mom, I'm all ready—now let me help you!

CHATTER CHATTER

Goo goo,
Ga ga,
W a a a a a a !

Mama Dada, Mama Dada,
Brrrooom! Bear! Baa!

No! Juice! Mine! More!
All gone! Cheese!
Ring around the roses.
Read again please!

ALL MY OWN WORK

Look! There's a rainbow , there's a house , flowers , chimneys , a fence , a mouse . And those are clouds whooshing across the sky . That's a cat . That's a swing , all my friends, me in the middle .

I've made you a present as fine as can be.
It's all my own work. And look! Signed by me.

13

TWISTY-TURNY TROUSERS

My shirt is dangling on my head,
my undies are in a twist.
My socks are flapping off my feet,
my shoe is on my fist.

My trousers are twisty-turny,
my left leg's in the right.
My head is in the armhole,
why are my clothes so tight?

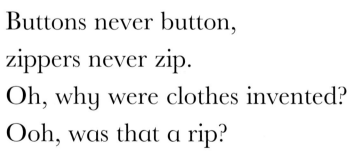

Buttons never button,
zippers never zip.
Oh, why were clothes invented?
Ooh, was that a rip?

Never mind. . . .

14

Right leg in right leg,
that seems to be okay.
Goodness me, it's working—

Hip, Hip, Hip, Hurray!

NO MORE NAPS

No nap! No nap!
I want to play.
I've far too many things to do
to sleep the day away.
Rock   Rock   Rock

No nap! No nap!
I want to eat.
I'm perfectly wide awake
and waiting for a treat.
Yum   Yum   Yum

No nap! No nap!
I want to watch TV.
Who wants to lie there in a bed
and snooze away, not me!
Yak   Yak   Yak

No nap! No nap!
I'm bouncy as can be.
Look! Here's my best book.
Let's read—first you, then me.
Read   Read   Read

But one day . . .

Rock Rock Rock

Yak Yak Yak

Yum Yum Yum

Read Read Read

I did it! No more naps for me!

SLIPPY-SLIDY BEANS

Why bother with a knife and fork
when fingers do it better?
It's silly shoveling scrambled eggs
splat all down my sweater.

If I try to cut a cake
or chop a bean in two,
that food goes sliding off the plate—
my only hope is glue.

I try so hard to use a fork,
but it just can't be done.
Stop wriggling, noodle!
Get back here, pea!
Oh no, not another bit of food
sliding down my knee!

Wait a minute.
There's a bean on my fork.
Careful now. . . .
Slowly does it . . . open wide. . . .
Ohhhhhhhhhhhhhh—
YES! Easy-peasy, really.

19

ZOOM WOBBLE WOBBLE

Z o o m Wobble Wobble . . .

W a a a a a a !

Z o o m Wobble Wobble . . .

CRASH!

Z o o m

Wobble Wobble . . .

Z O O M !

TIP-TOP TOWER

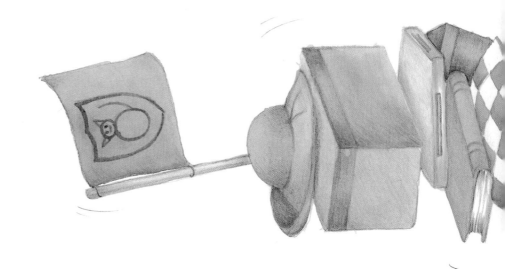

We're building a tip-top tower

high above our heads.

A multi-storied tower

in browns and blues and reds.

Add a stool,

toss a hat,

pile on bricks.

No! Not the cat!

We're almost there.

Let's add a flag

to make our tower tall.

Oh no! Oh help! Mind your heads!

I think it's going to fall!

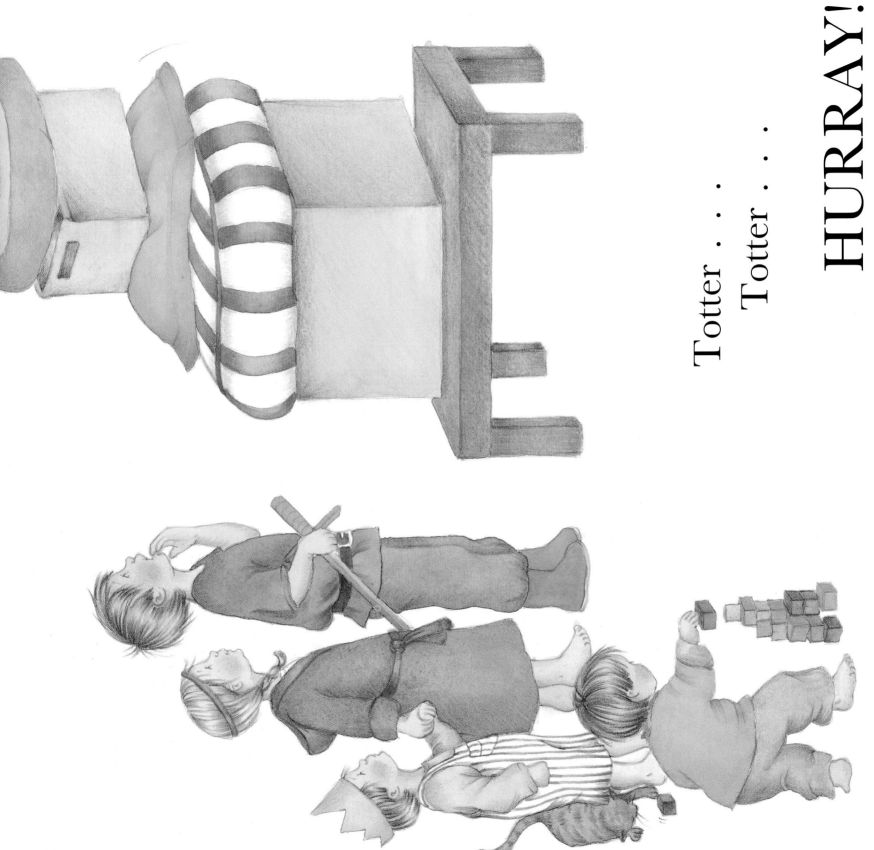

Totter . . . .
Totter . . . .
HURRAY!

23

I REMEMBER

I remember when that was my crib.
I remember when that was my chair.
I remember when that was my cup.
I remember when that was my bear.

24

I remember when that was my ball.
I remember when that was my swing.
I remember when that was my trike. . . .
Now our baby's got everything!

LOOK WHAT I CAN DO

I can hold a pencil.

I can tie my shoe.

I can paint a rainbow.

I can stick with glue.

I can plant some flowers.

I can make a face.

I can catch a snowflake.

I can win a race.

I can stand on tiptoe.
I can count to three.
I can splash in puddles.
I can climb a tree.

Oh clever, clever me!

I'M GROWING, IT'S SHOWING

I'm growing!
It's showing!
I can open the door!
When I stand on tiptoe, s t r e t c h and s t r e t c h
I can peep into the top drawer.

I'm growing!
It's showing!
I can touch the shelf!
Don't bring the chair . . . take away the stool—
I can reach it all by myself.

Yikes! It's high up here!

Now I am **tall.**

I used to be small.

AGAIN! AGAIN!

Again! Again!

Again! Again!

Again! Again!

Again! Again!

Again! Again! Again!

HOP SKIP JUMP

I can h^{o}p h^{o}p h^{o}p,

I can s$_{ki}$p s^{ki}p s$_{ki}$p,

See me j^{u}m$_p$ j^{u}m$_p$ j^{u}m$_p$,

Watch me z i p z i p z i p .

I can dance,

I can vault,

I can even s$_o$$_m$$_e$$_r$$_s$$_a$$_u$$_l$$_t$

Kick that ball,

roll that hoop!

With a shimmy shimmy shimmy

and a wh^{oo}p, wh$_{oo}$p-de-wh^{oo}p.

BOO-HOO! SHAMPOO!

I'm hiding on the sofa
beneath a toy or two.
I don't want Dad to find me
'cause I know what he will do.

"Yoo-hoo! Shampoo!"
"No! No shampoo!"
Dad says it won't sting,
but I know that isn't true.

Shampoo drips in your eyes
in great big gloopy globs.
Boo-hoo! I HATE SHAMPOO.
I cannot speak for sobs.

But Dad says it will be all right.
We'll make bubbles everywhere:
my back, my face, my chinny-chin-chin,
and even in my hair.

CRIB TO BED

My toes are poking out.
My knees are scrunched up by my head.
I can't move,
I'm squashed in so tight.
Time I switched to a bed!

I tiptoe to the big-boy bed
and sneak beneath the sheet.
There's so much room to roll around
and loads of space for feet.

Trouble is, I feel lost—
this bed is awfully wide.
I'll just wiggle around until I . . .

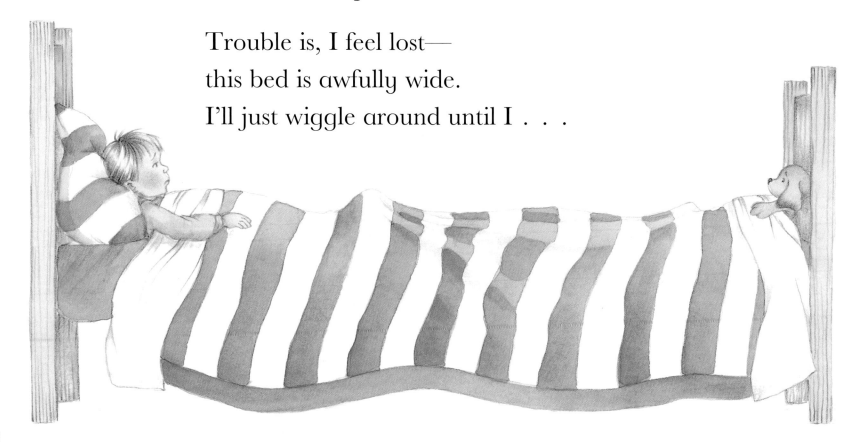

Ahhh! I'm sliding off the side!
Grab hold of Dog,
yank on the sheet.
Oh no! I'm falling out!

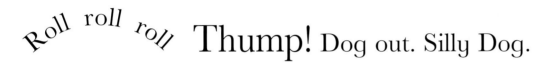

Roll roll roll Thump! Dog out. Silly Dog.

Roll roll roll Bump! Silkie out. Silly Silkie.

Roll roll roll Thump! Bump! Silly me.

One night I'll get it right!

GOOD-NIGHT, SLEEP TIGHT

Good-night Hedgie.
Good-night Bear.
Good-night Dolly.
Good-night Hare.
Good-night Silkie.
Good-night Frog.
Good-night Little Rooster.
Good-night Spotty Dog.

No more noise,
not a peep.
Close your eyes.
It's time to sleep.

Good-night
Sleep tight
S h h h h h

Sleep